Amazing New World Animals

Illustrated by Donna Freitag
Written by BStieferman
Front cover colored by BStieferman

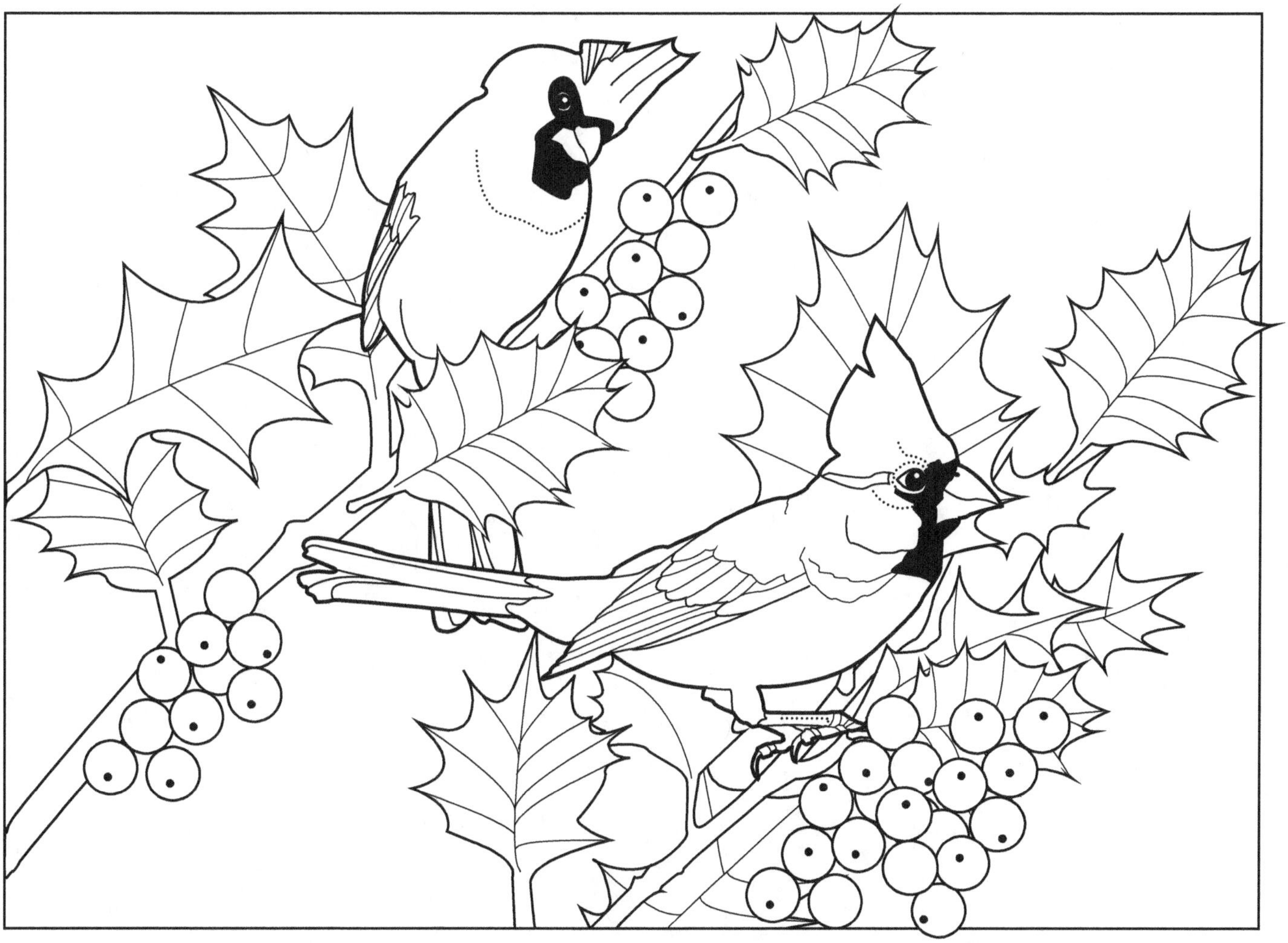

DONNAFREITAG.COM

How to color this book

Amazing New World Animals is a coloring book for adults. You'll enjoy hours of creative, relaxing, stress relieving fun as you color 27 all new animal designs. All are beautiful, new, original artwork never before seen in any collection.

Coloring Tips

Colored pencils are the most popular way to color. It's best to get a large set of at least 48 colors. Some of the best brands are Prismacolor and Staedtler.

In addition, you'll need an eraser and a good pencil sharpener. Also popular are markers. Warning: they tend to bleed through the page. So if you use them, place a sheet or thick paper underneath so the ink doesn't leak onto the picture below. Copic markers are a great brand.

Marker sets offer a smaller choice of colors than pencil sets. That's one reason why the pro colorists often use a combination of pencils, markers, gel pens and even crayons.

It all depends on the effects you want to produce.

Please post photos of your artwork on my Facebook page. I'd love to see what you've done!

In This Coloring Book, Relive the Magic When the Jesuits Discovered New World Animals

By BStieferman

In the 17th Century, upon entering the New World, the first explorers were petrified by the discovery of a variety of animals. In fact, ancient religious manuscripts described terrifying New World animals that will make your jaw drop.

What are these animals? A simple example is in an excerpt written by Father Paul Le Jeune concerning his time among the Montagnais. He writes of an animal that is not known to anyone born and raised in France:

"The other is a low animal, about the size of a little dog or cat. I mention it here, not on account of its excellence, but to make it a symbol of sin. I have seen three or four of them. It has black fur, quite beautiful and shining; and has upon its back two perfectly white stripes, which join near the neck and tail making an oval which adds greatly to their grace. The tail is bushy and well furnished with hair, like the tail of a fox; it carries it curled back like that of a squirrel. It is more white than black; and at first glance, you would say, especially when it walks that it ought to be called Jupiter's little dog. But it is so stinking and casts so foul an odor, that it is unworthy of being called the dog of Pluto. No sewer ever smelled so bad. I would not have believed it if I had not smelled it myself. Your heart almost fails you when you approach the animal; two have been killed in our court, and several days afterward there was a dreadful odor throughout our house that we could not endure it. I believe the sin smelled by Sainte Catherine de Sienne must have had the same vile odor" (Le Jeune, p. 70).

Father Le Jeune is describing none other than an Illinois native: The skunk.
The cow with a flat face: The Bison.
Skin folds up neatly, and spread out when in flight: The flying squirrel.

Jesuits. (1901). *The Jesuit relations and allied documents: Travels and explorations of the Jesuit missionaries in New France, 1610-1791: the original French, Latin, and Italian texts, with English translations and notes.* R. G. Thwaites (Ed.). Cleveland, OH: Burrows Bros. Co.

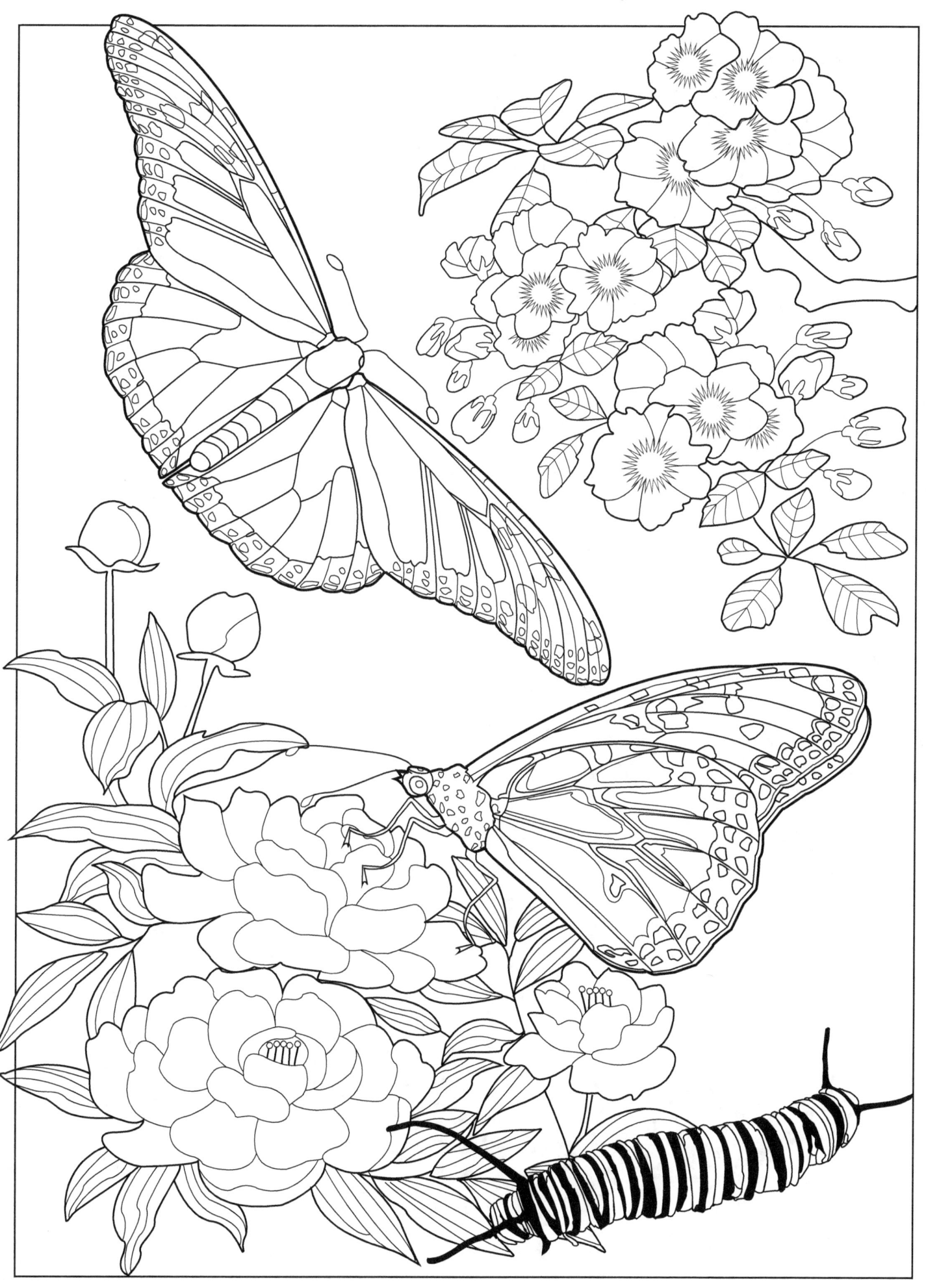

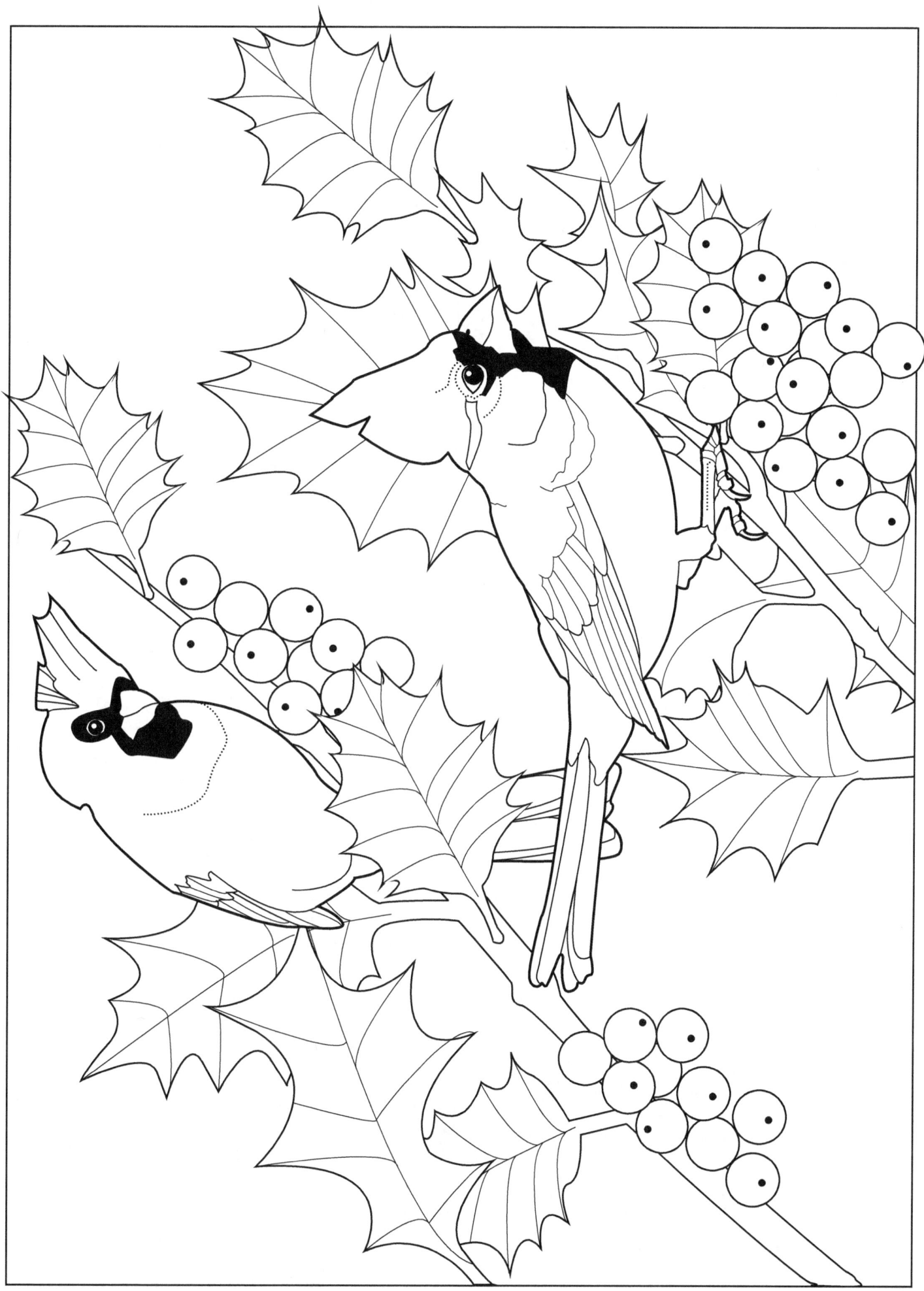

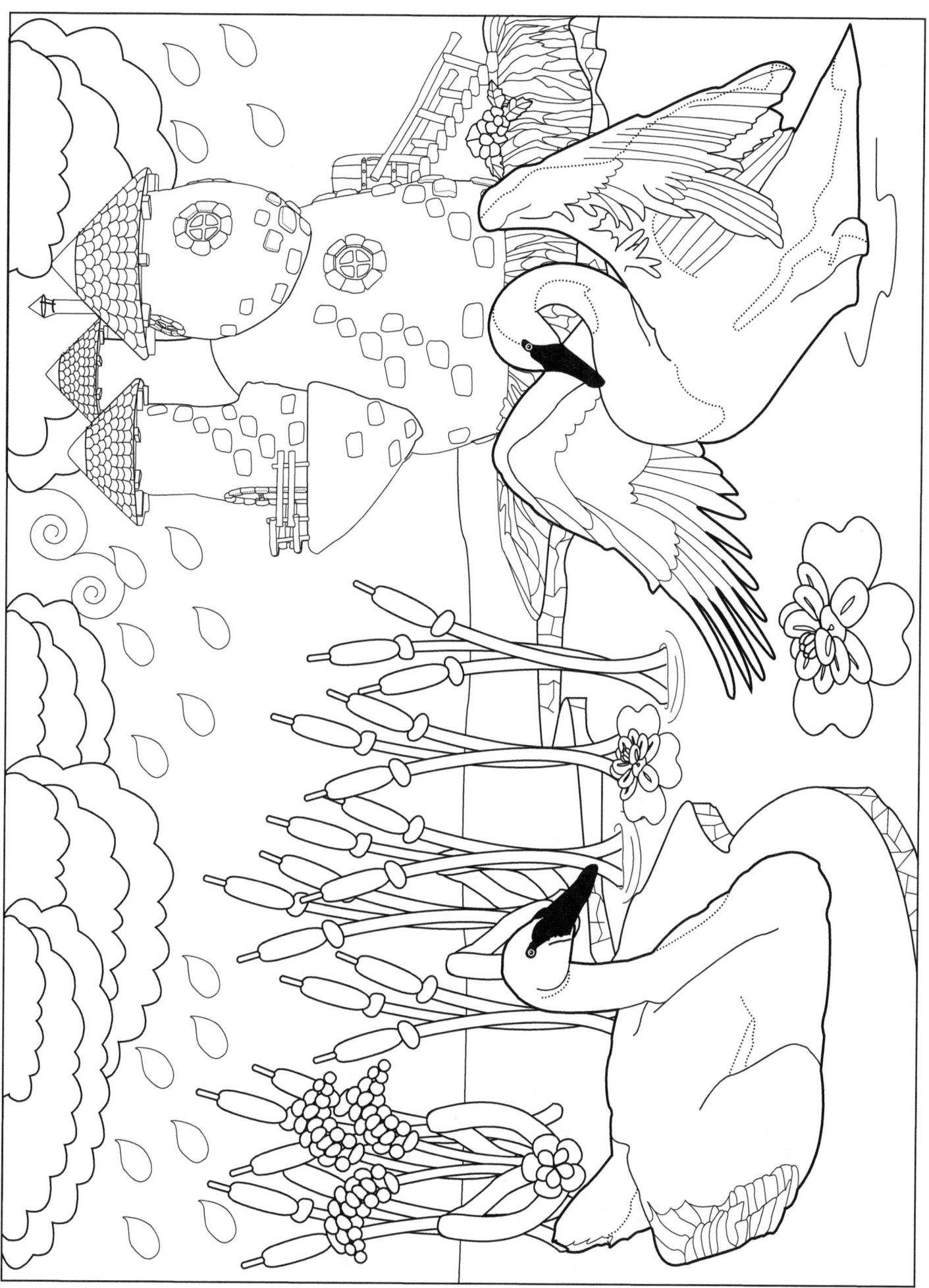

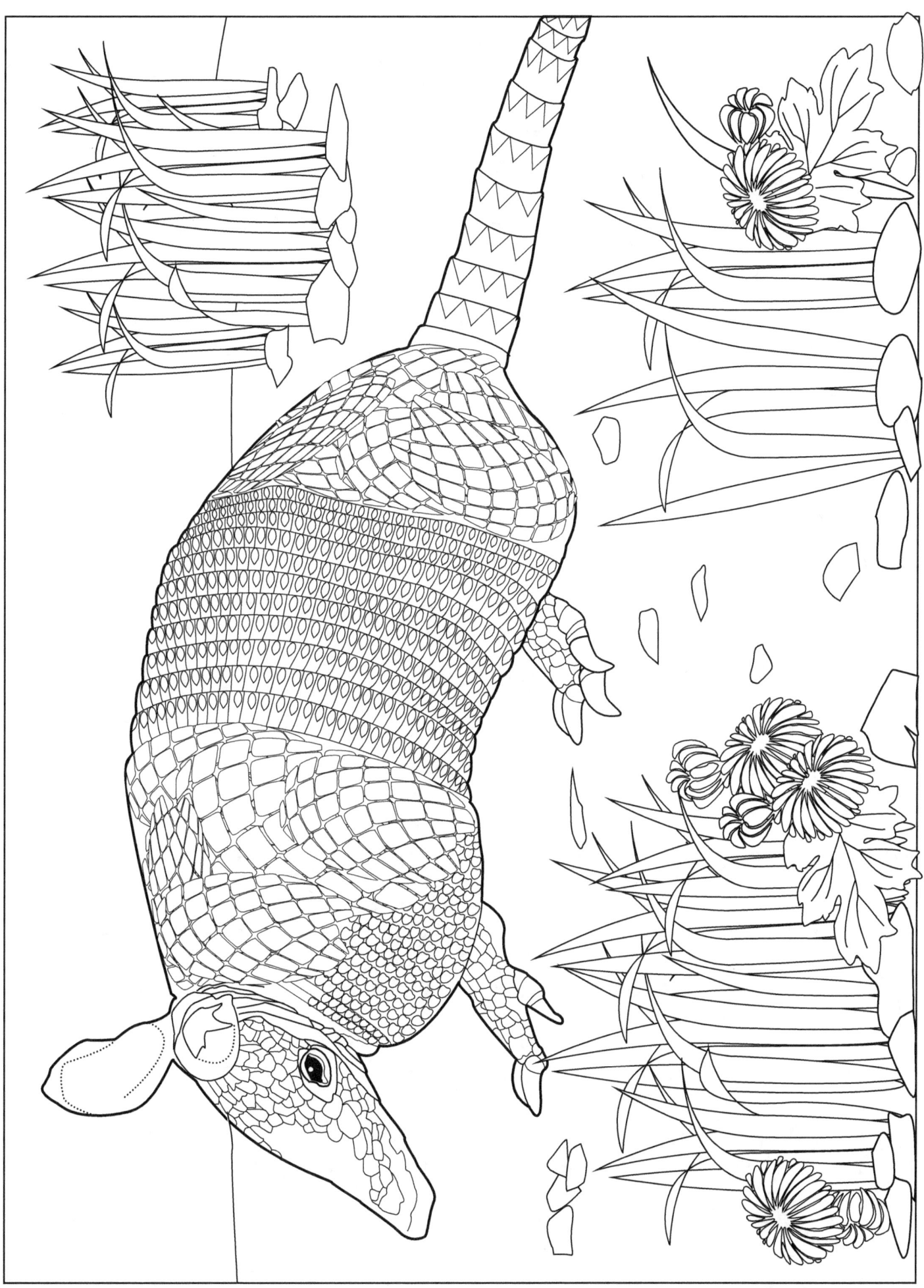

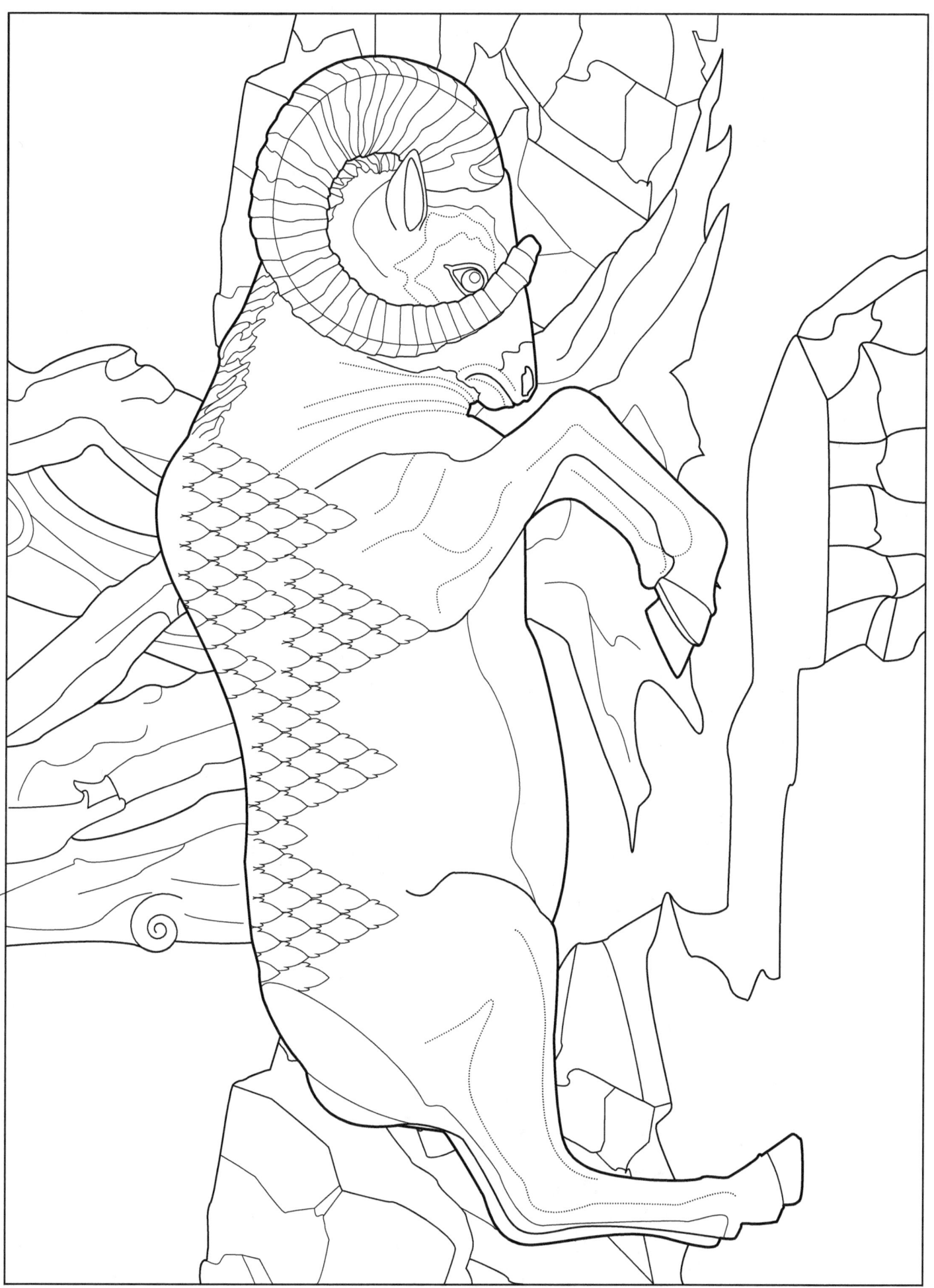

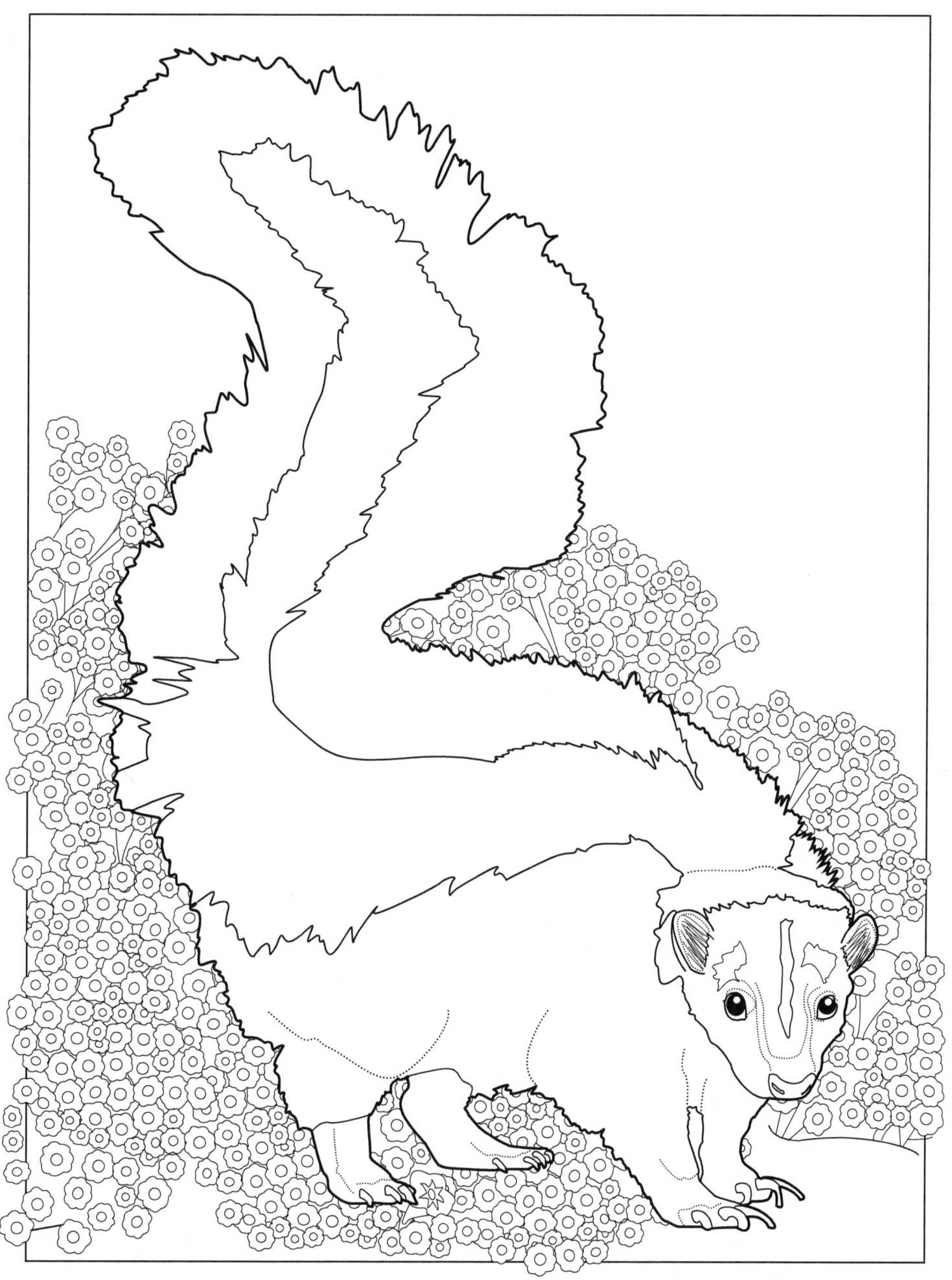

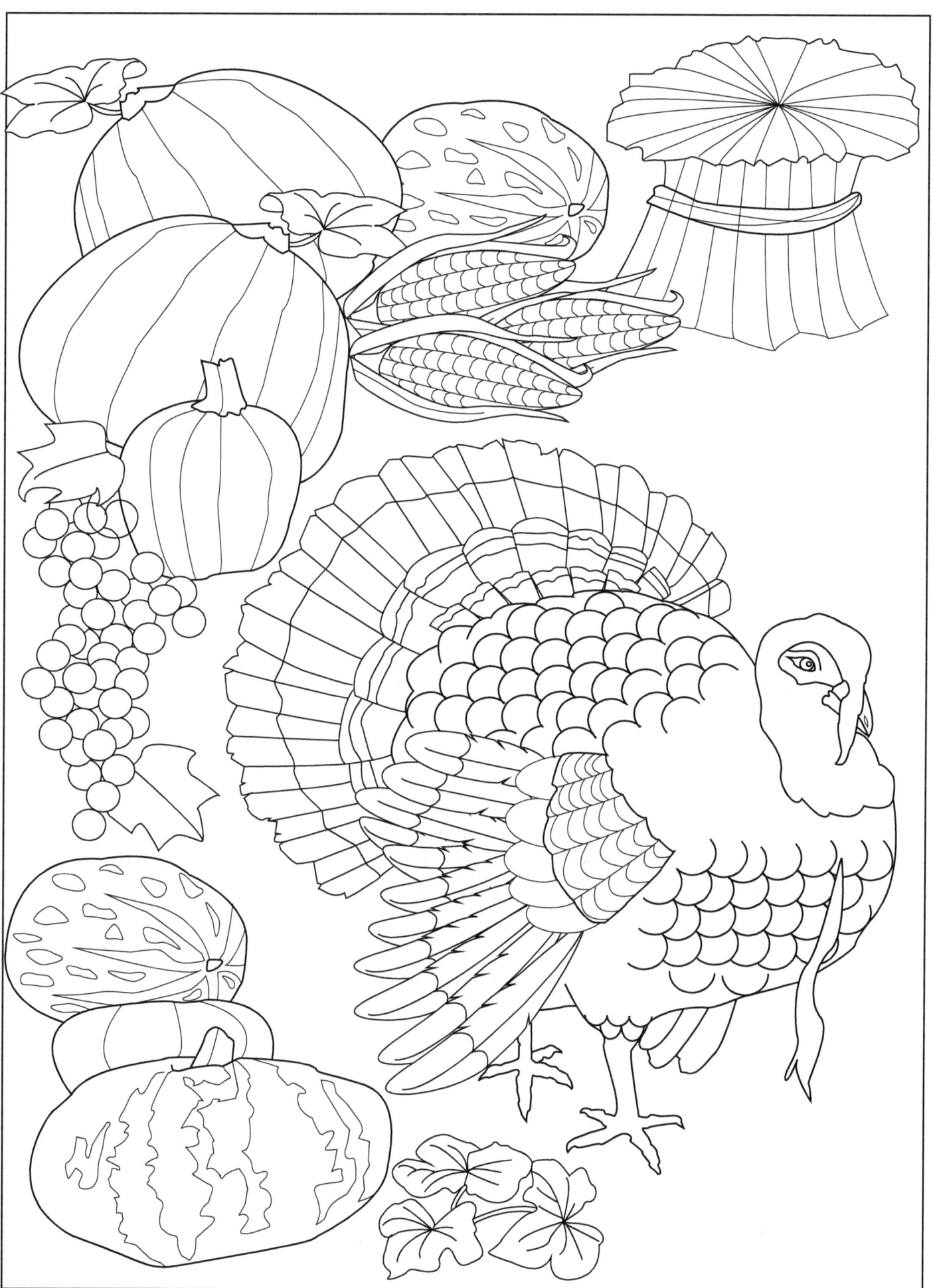

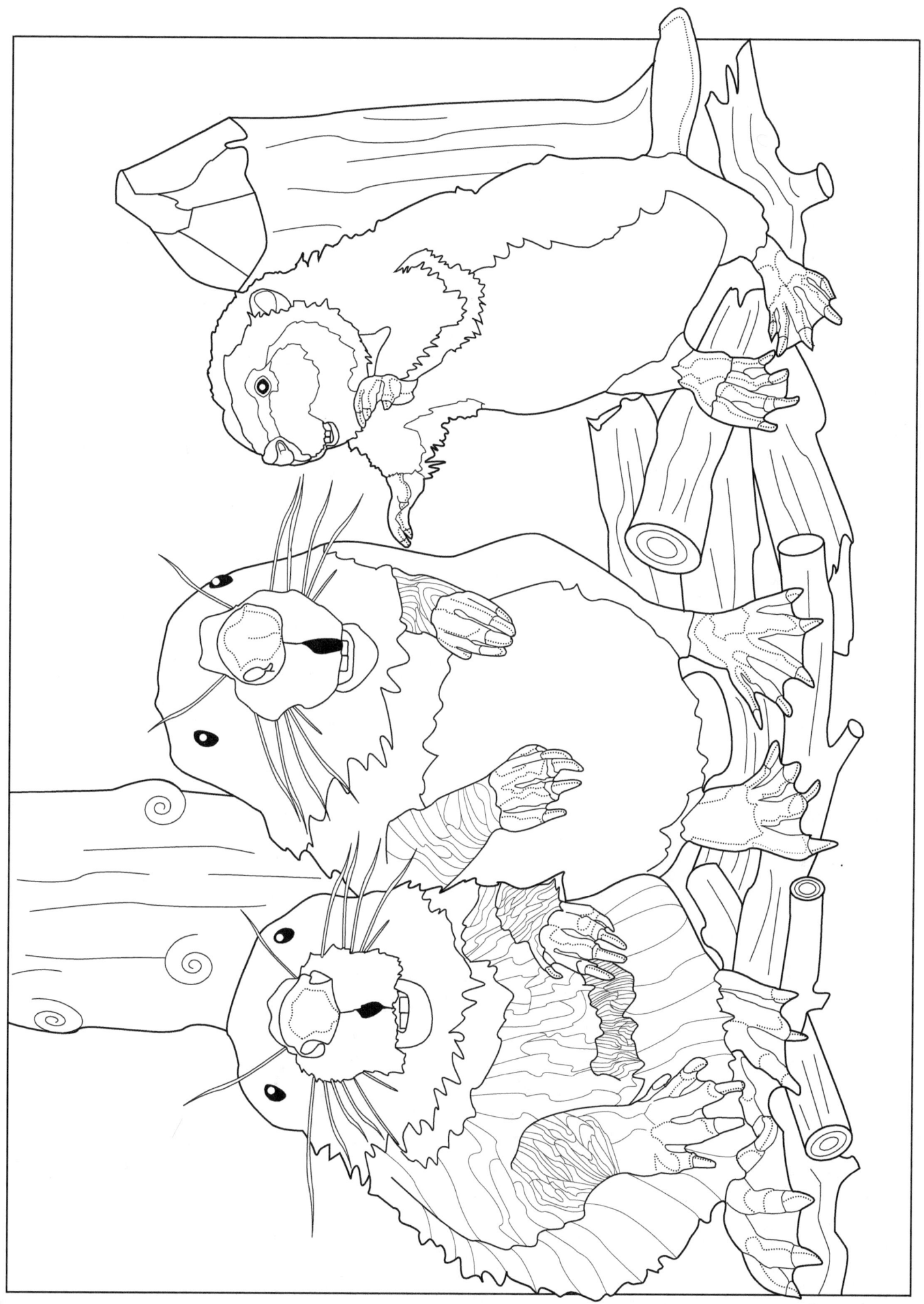

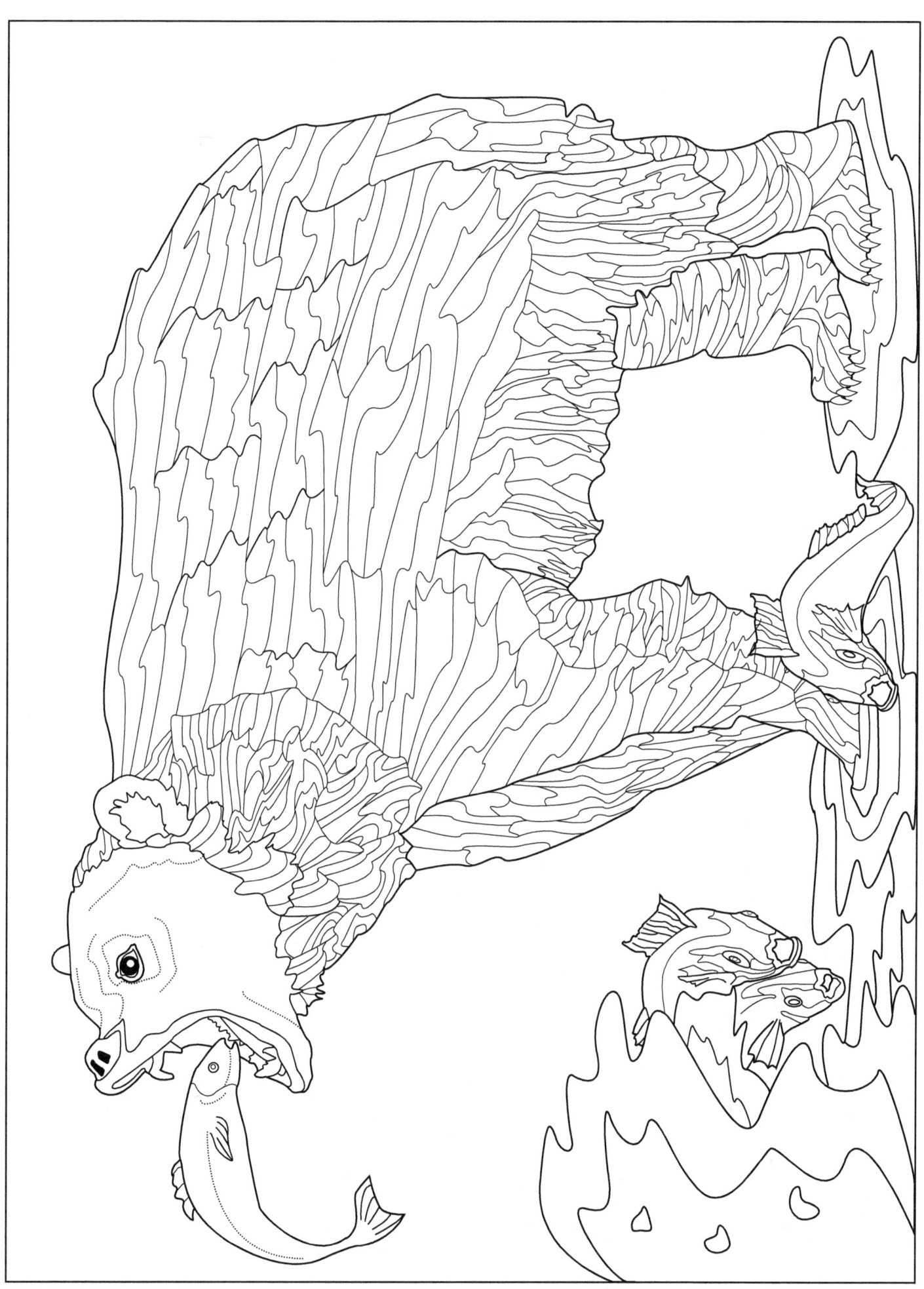

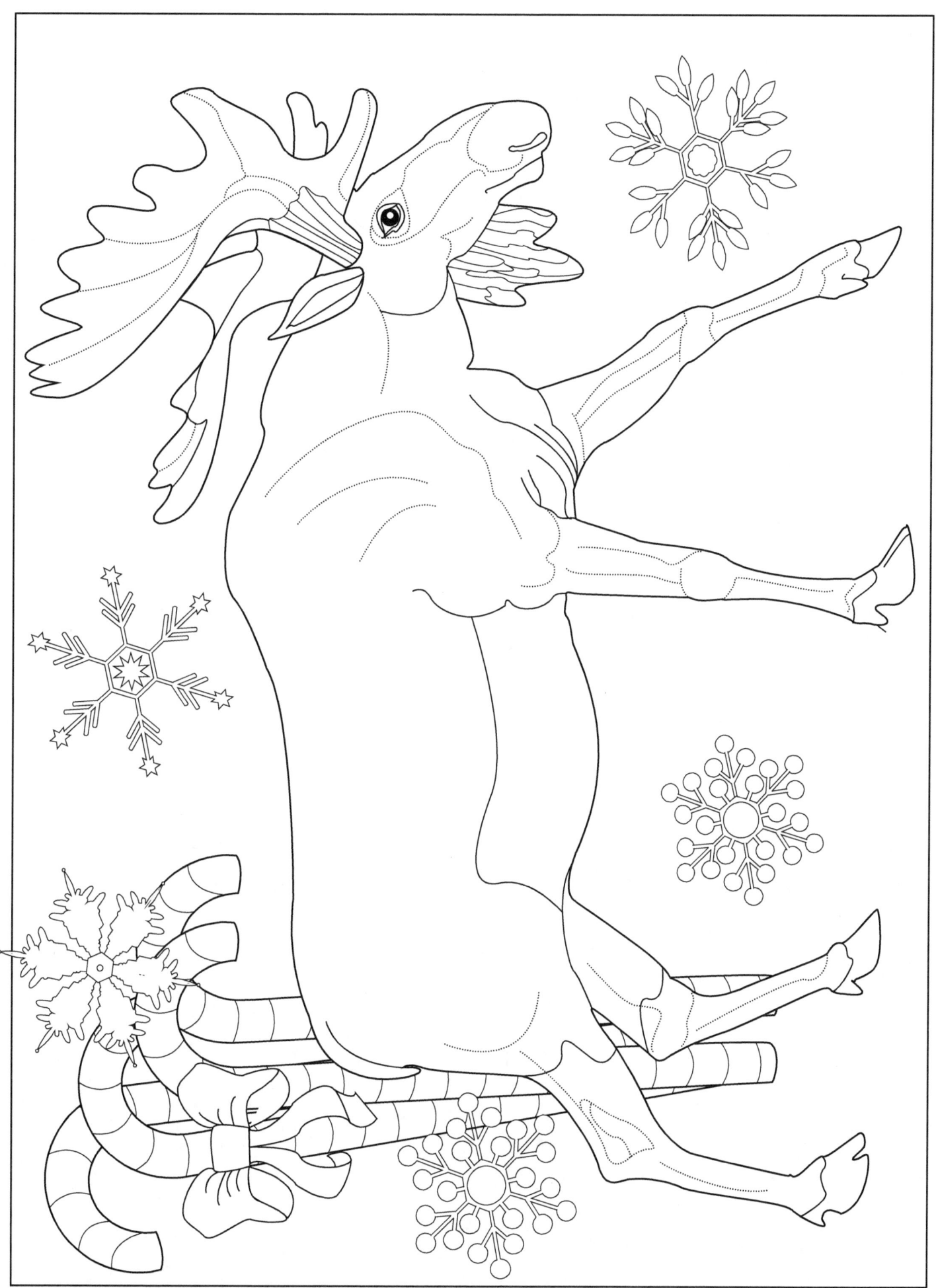

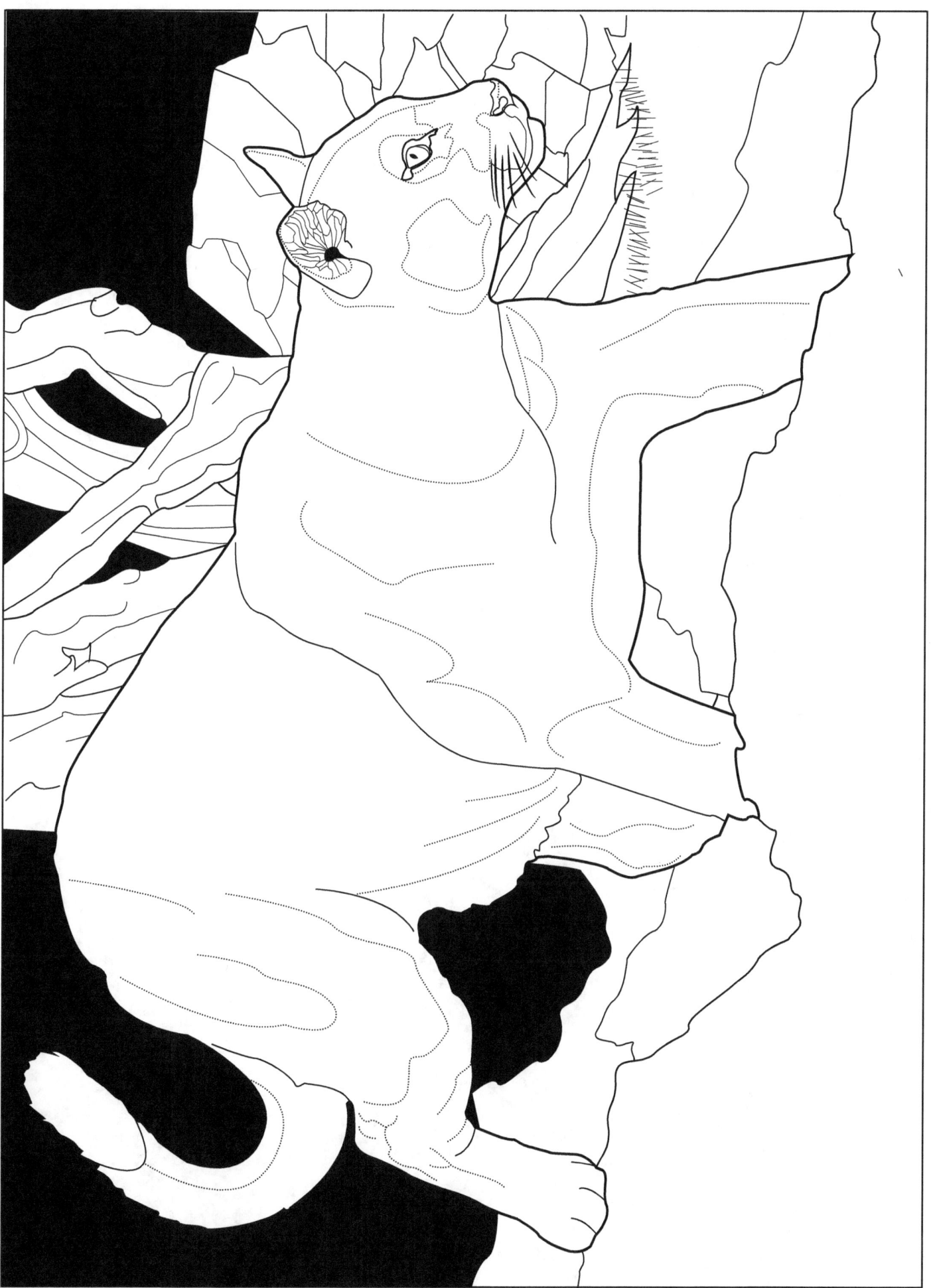

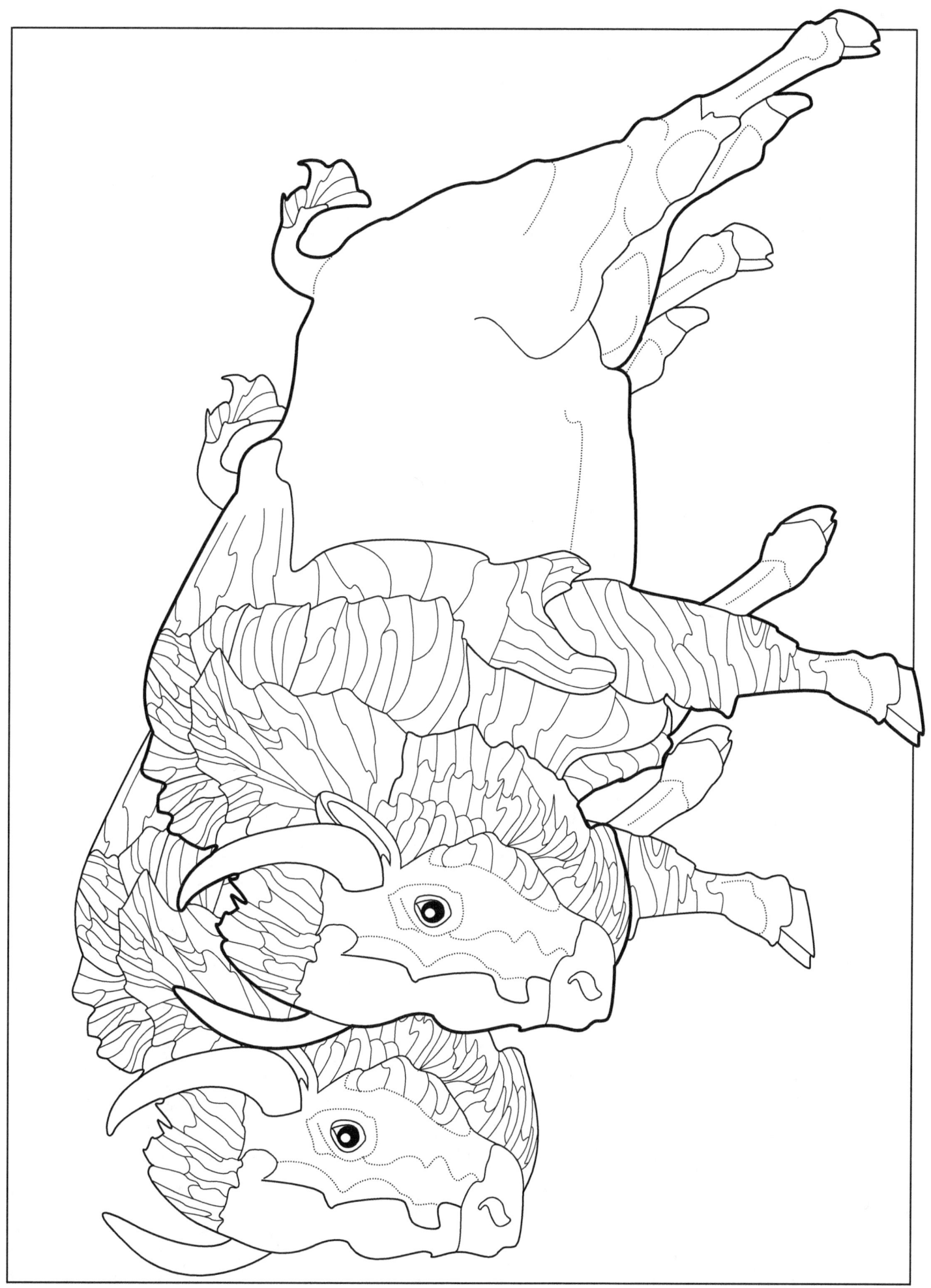

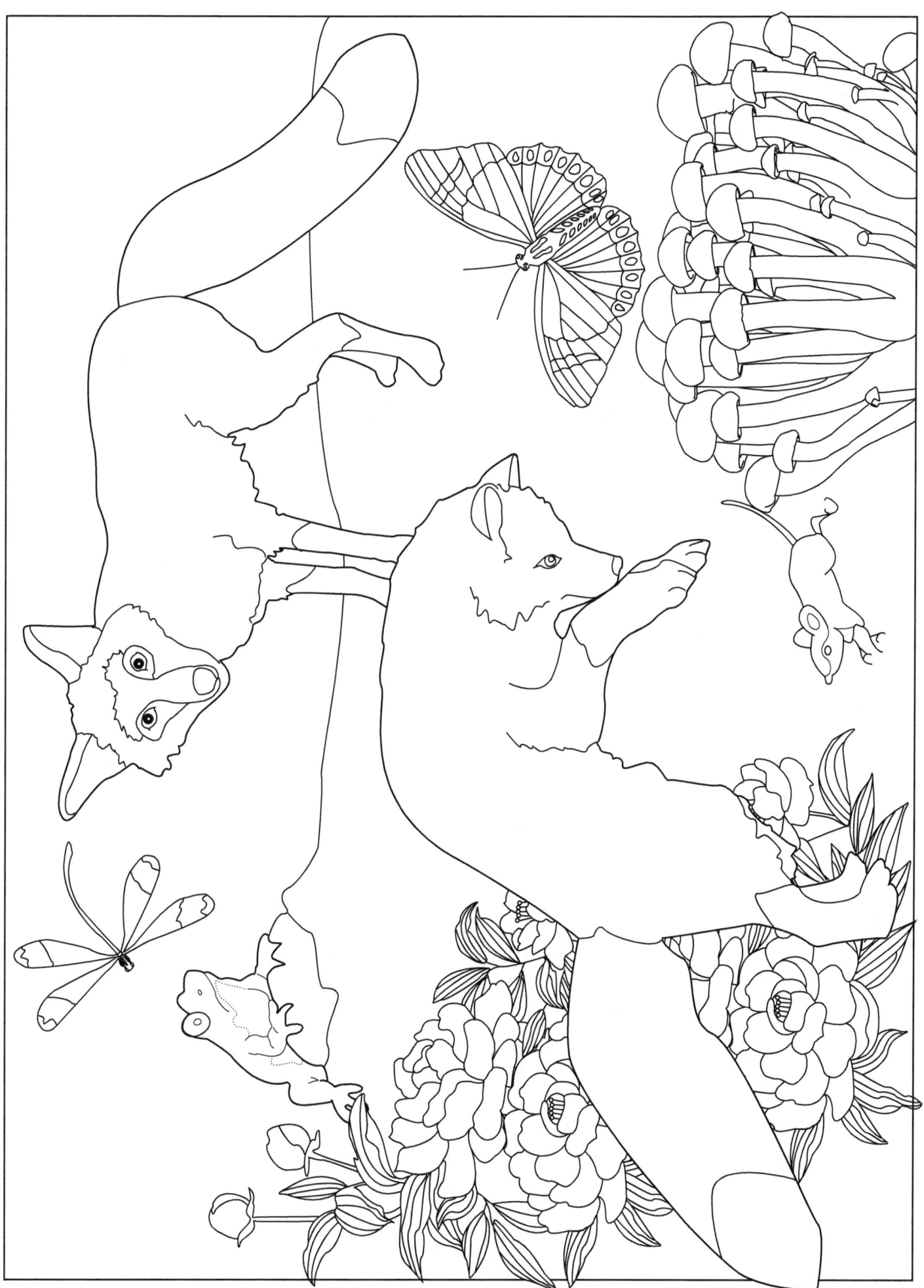

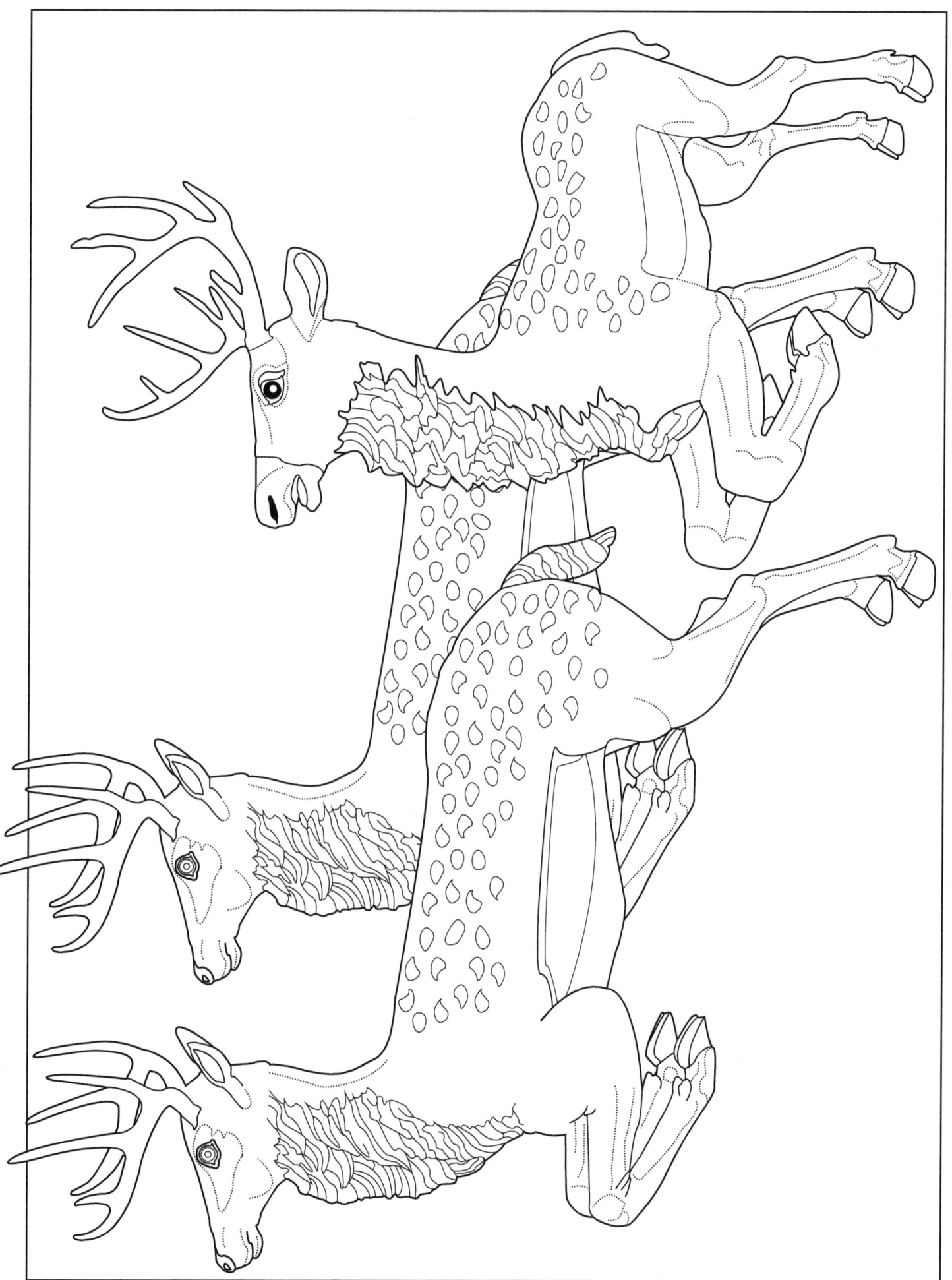

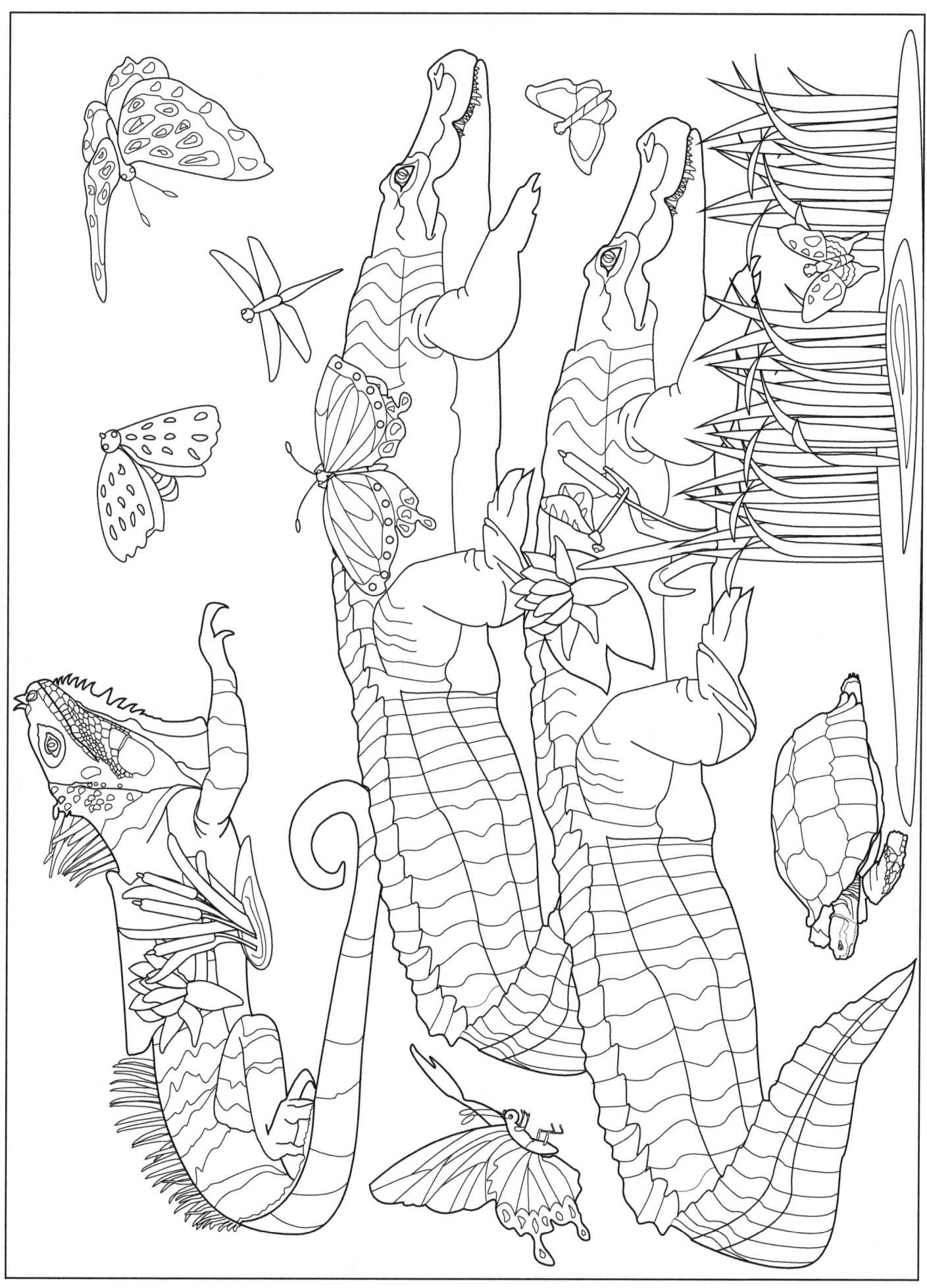

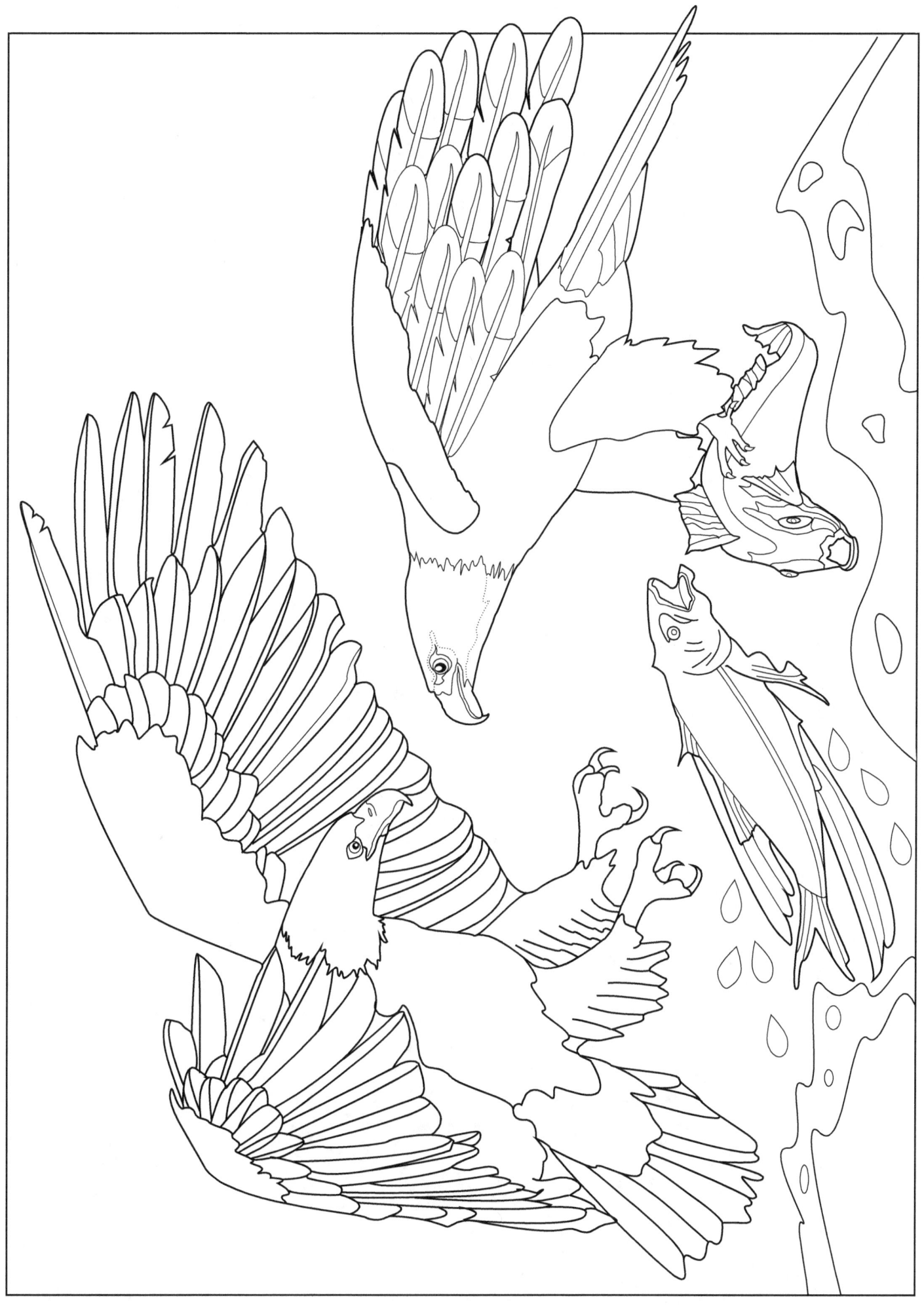

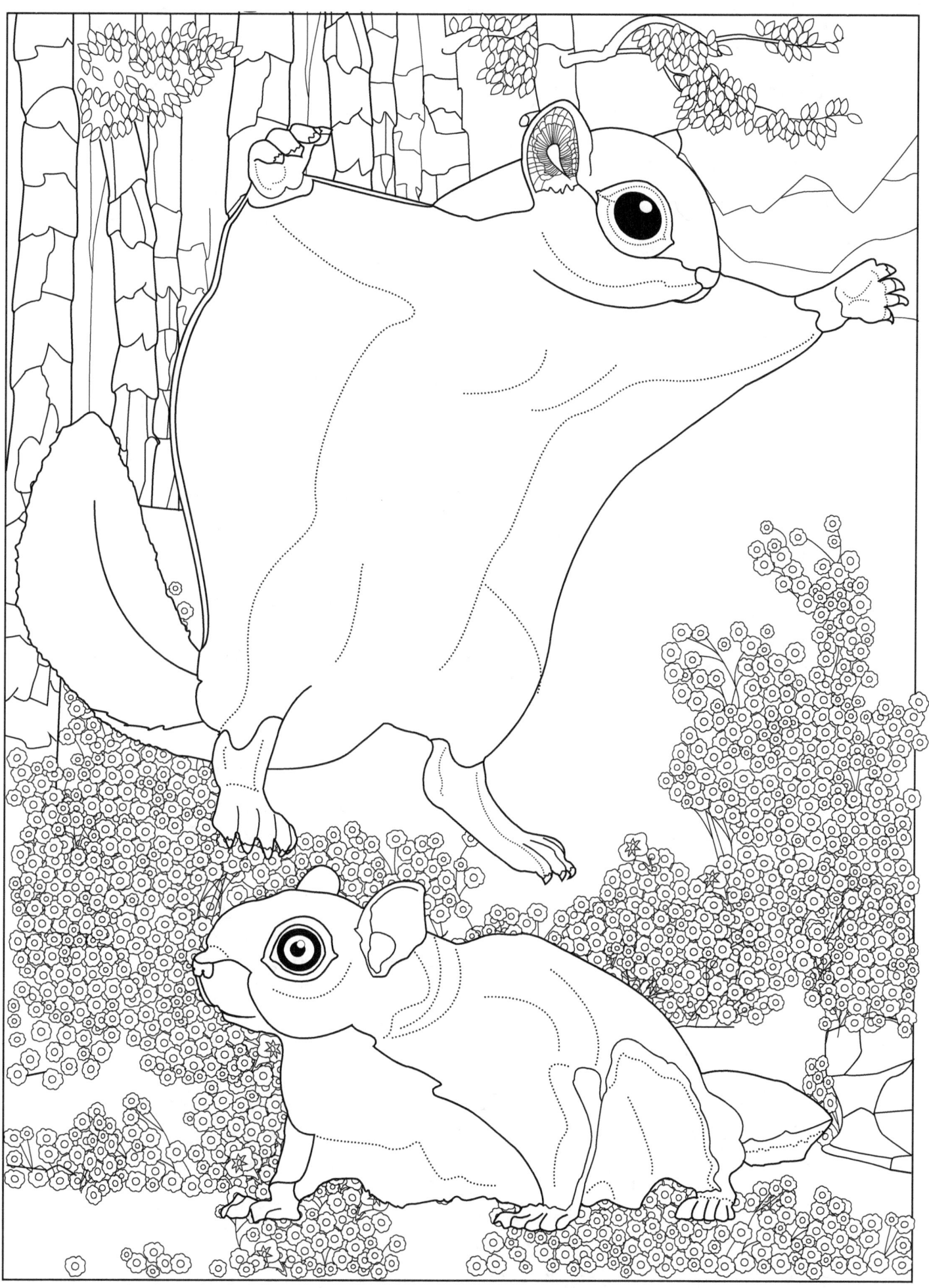

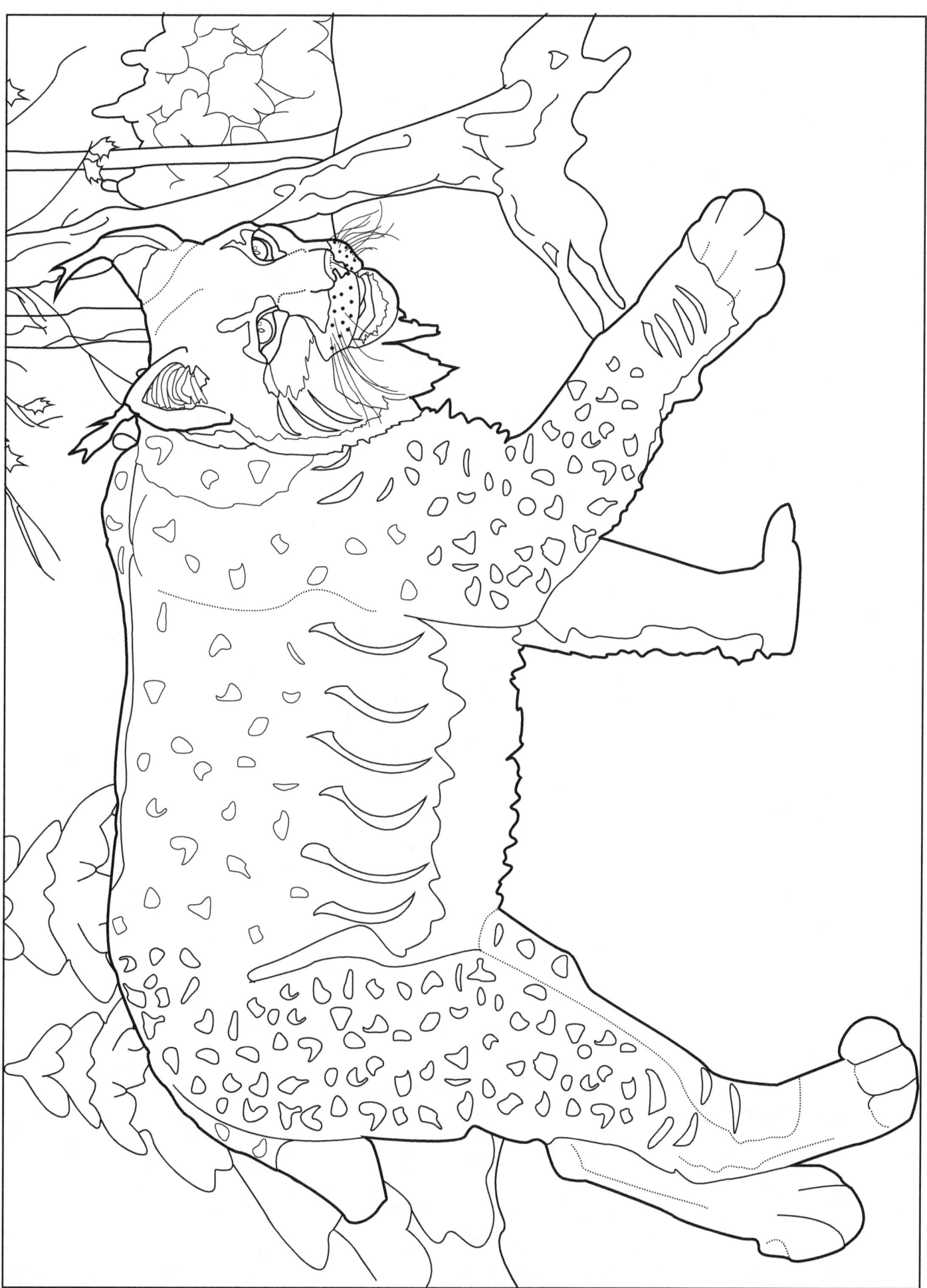

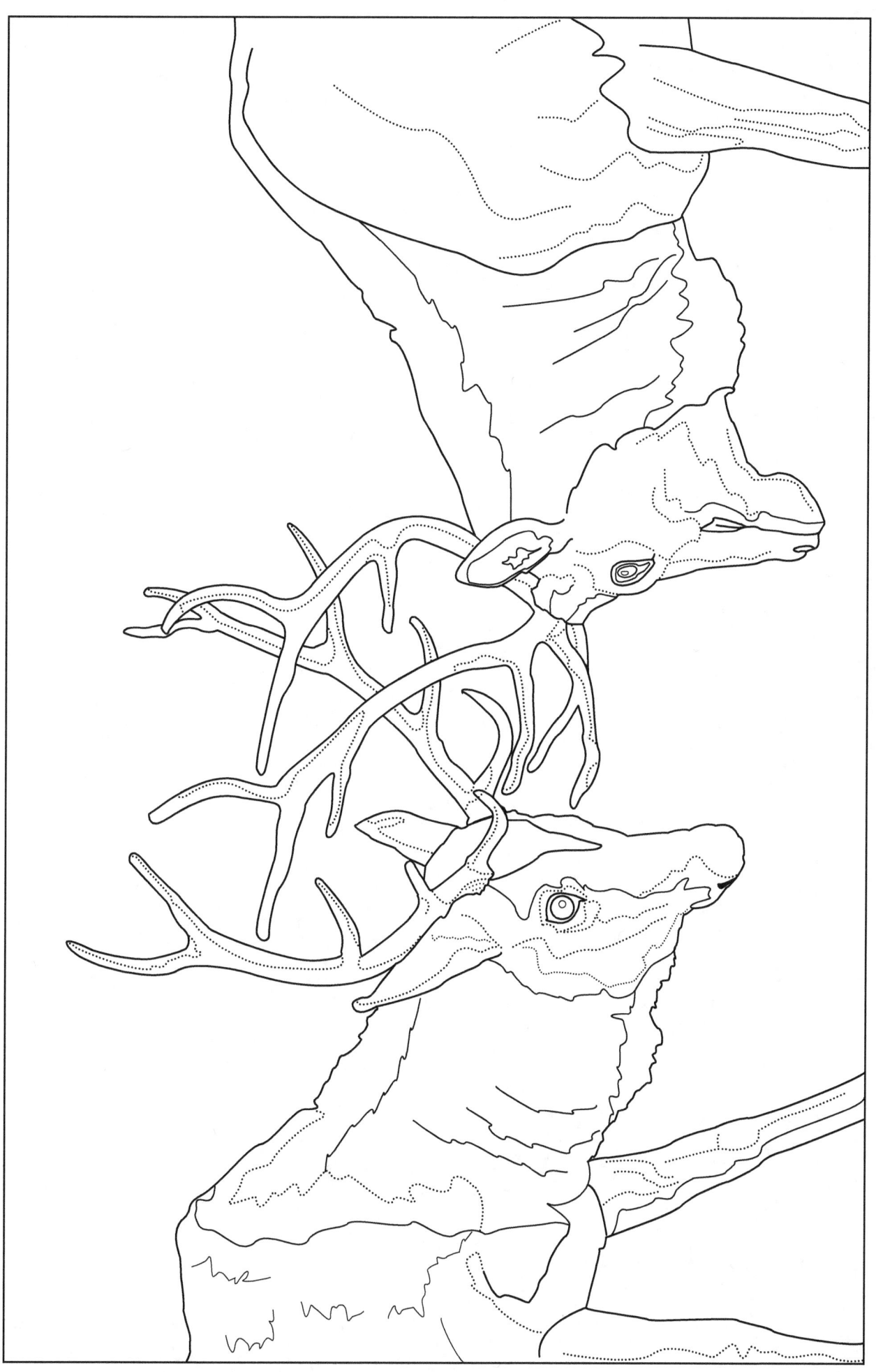

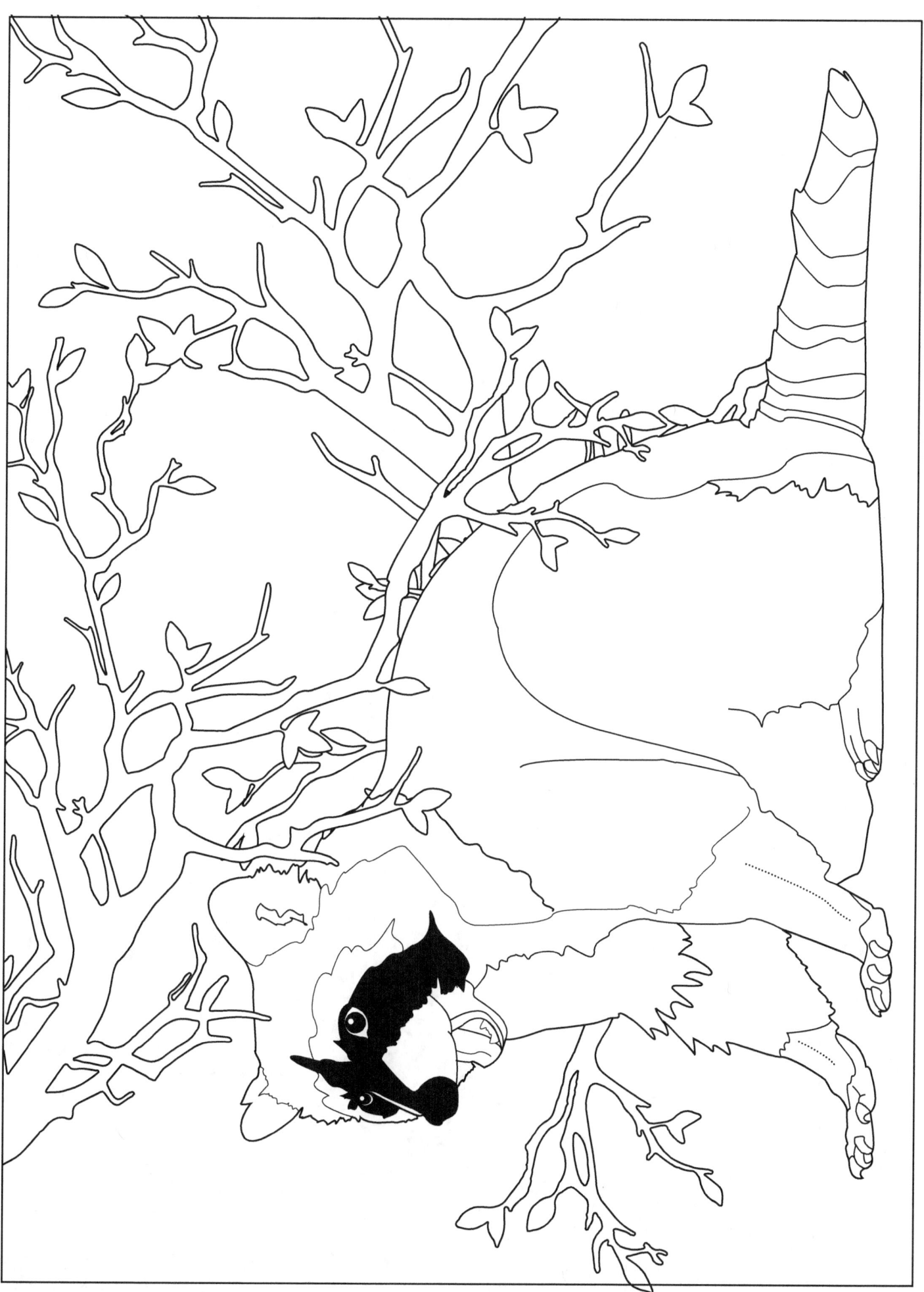

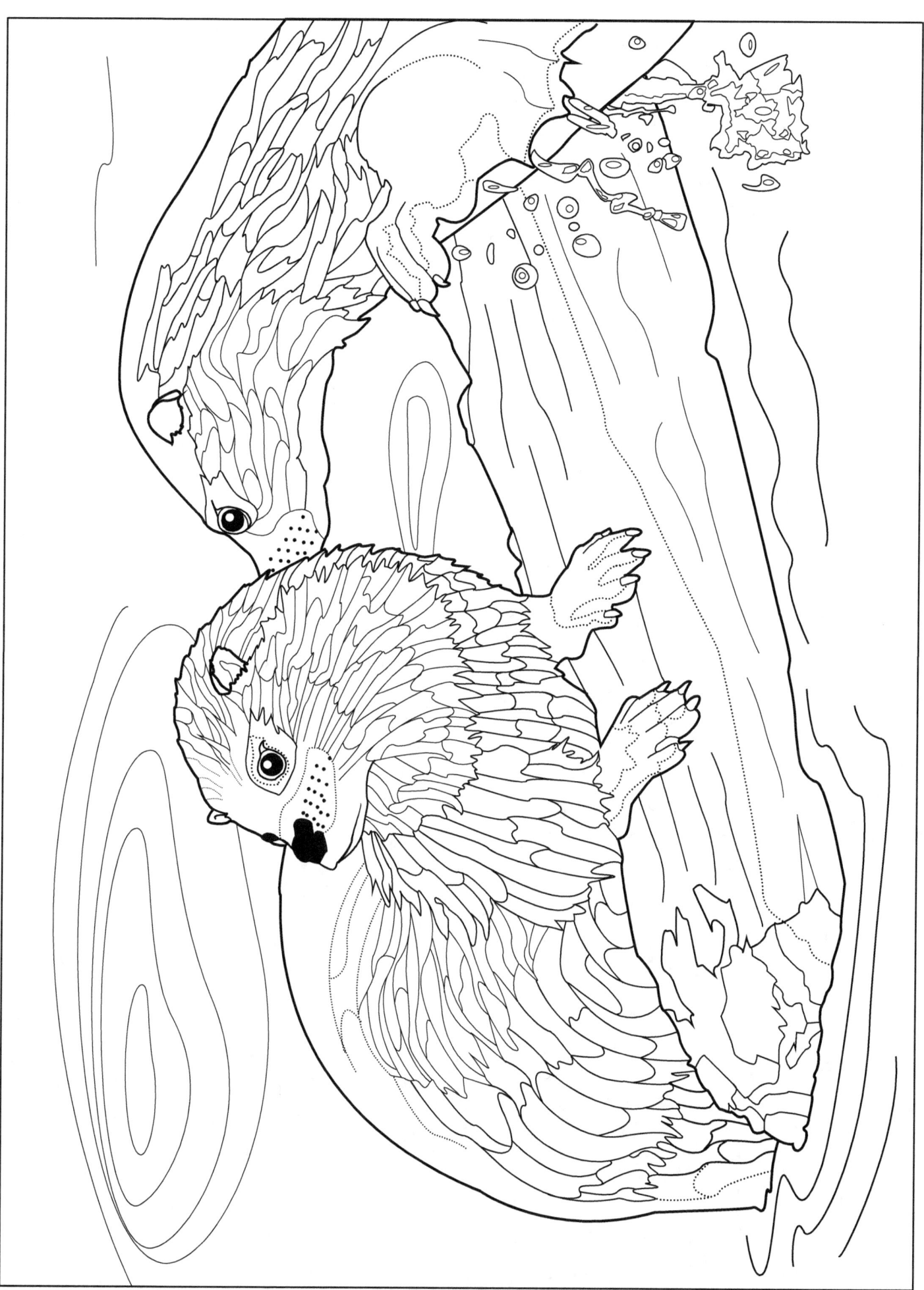

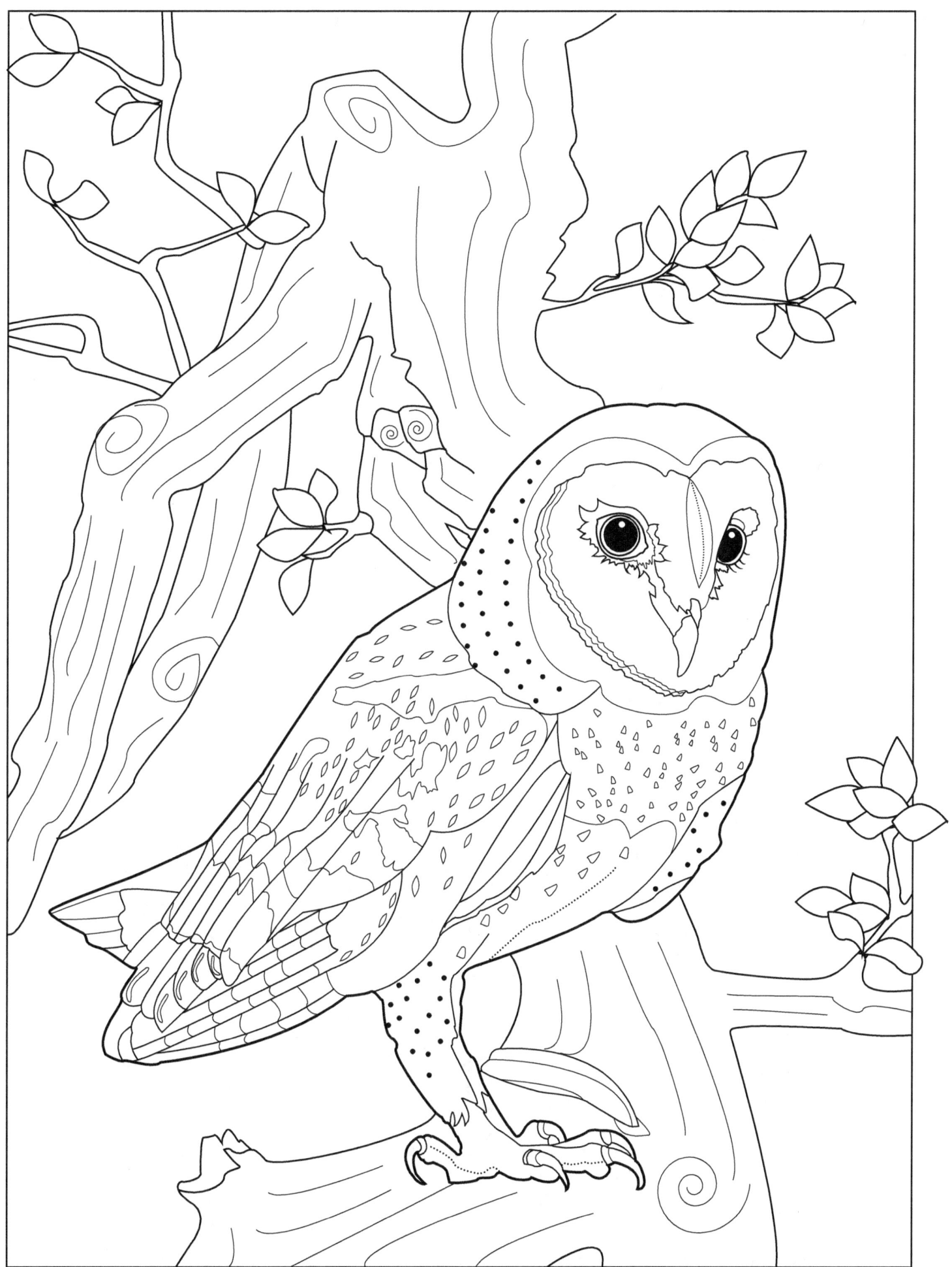

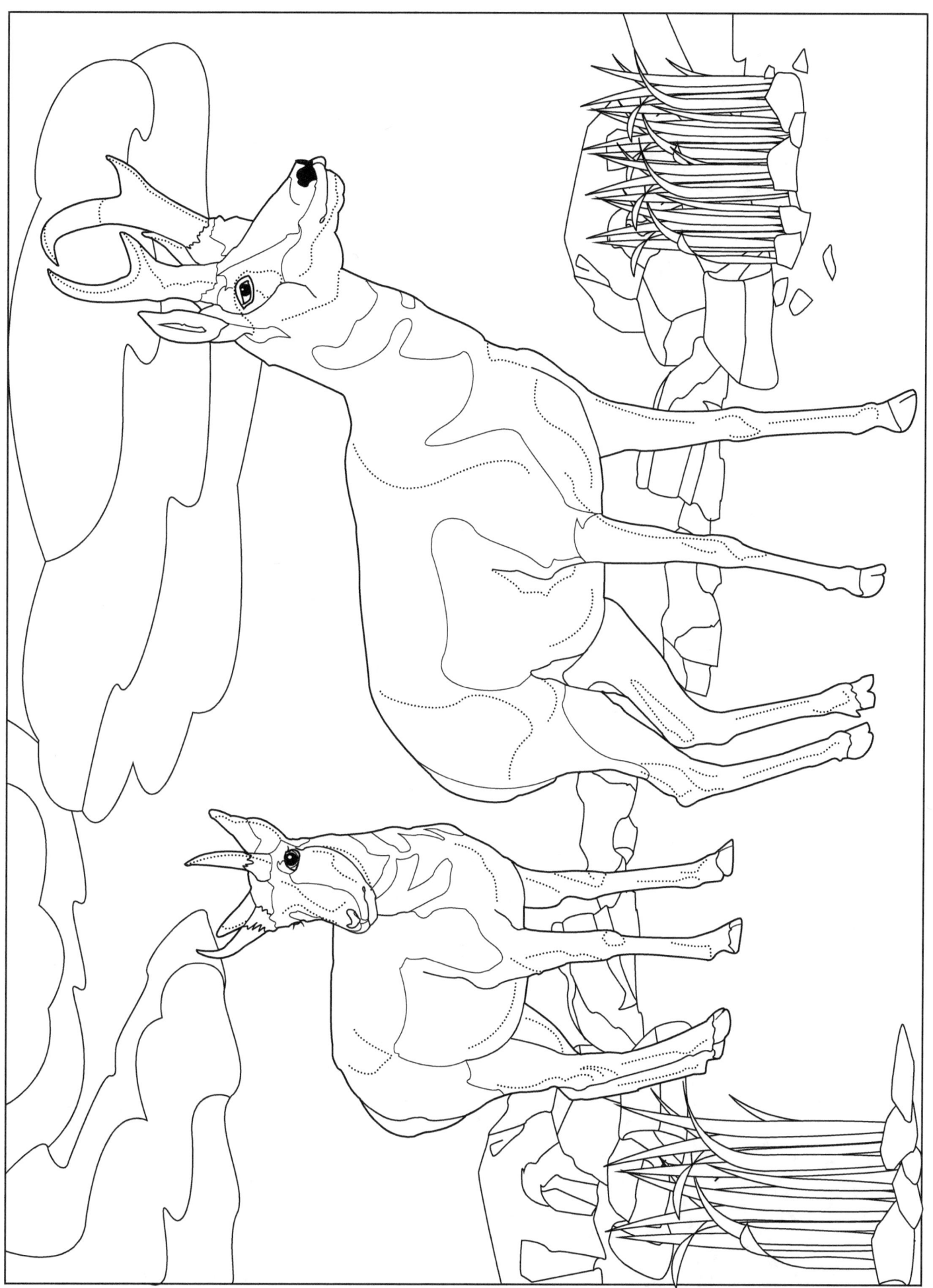

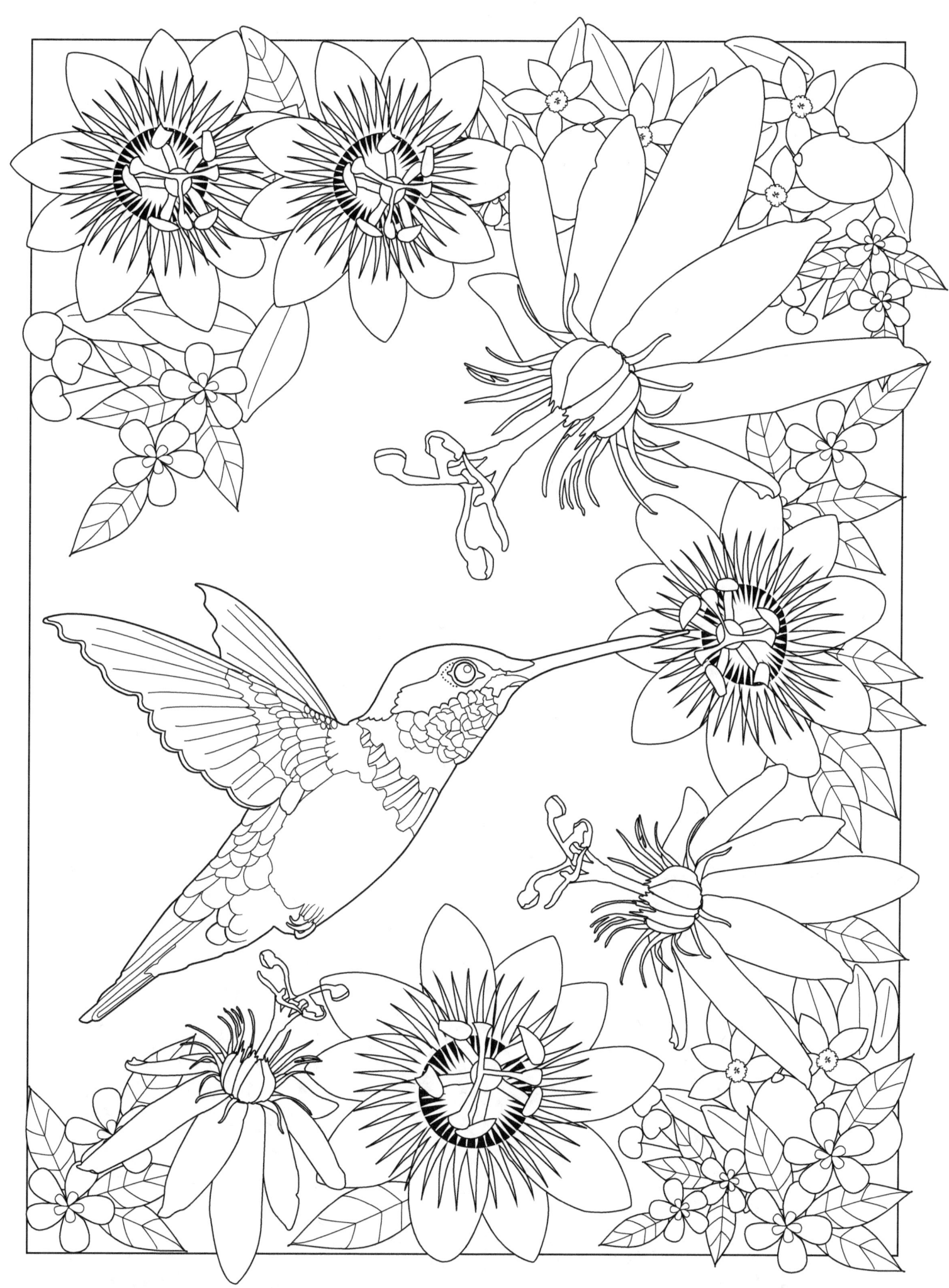

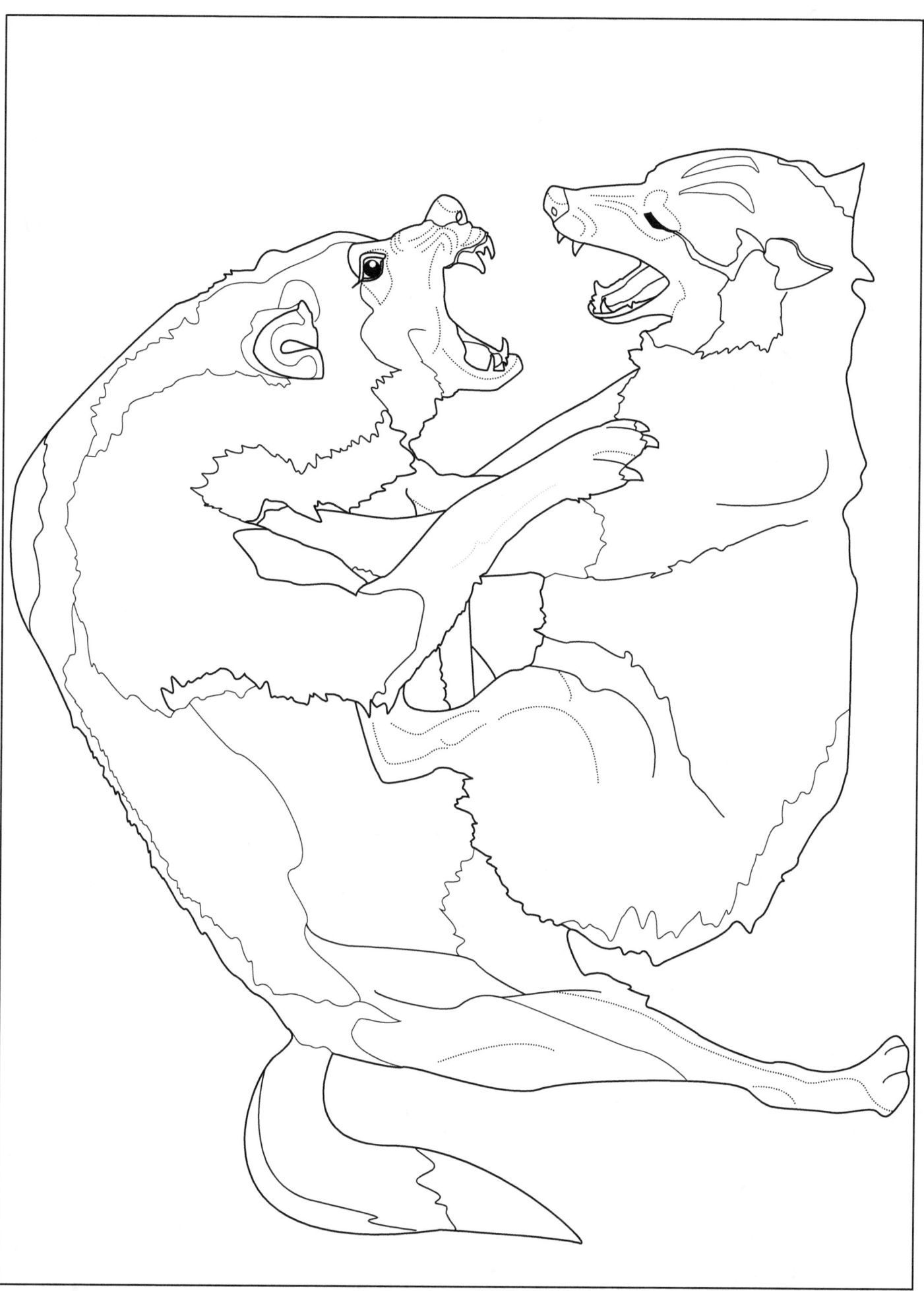

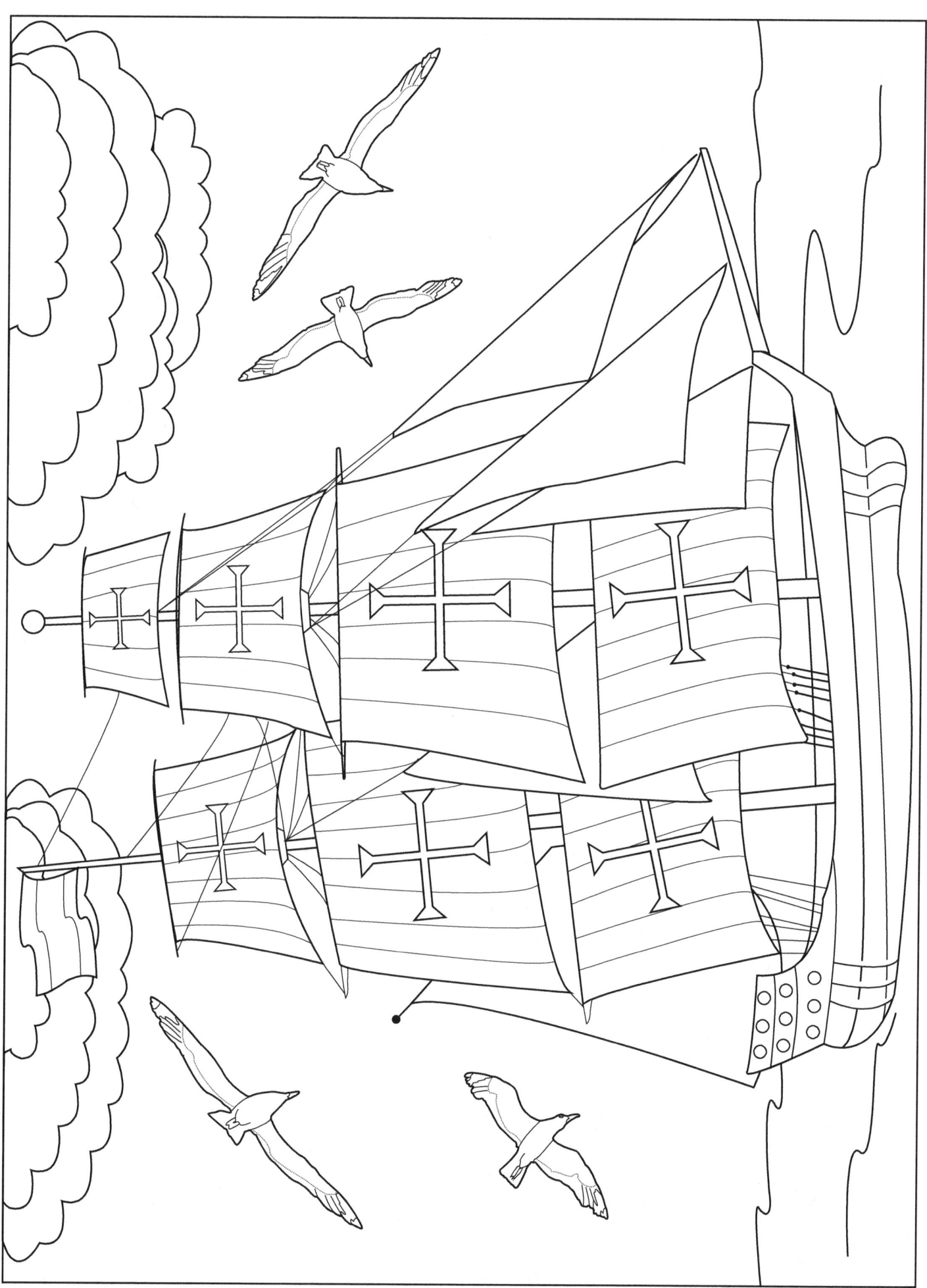

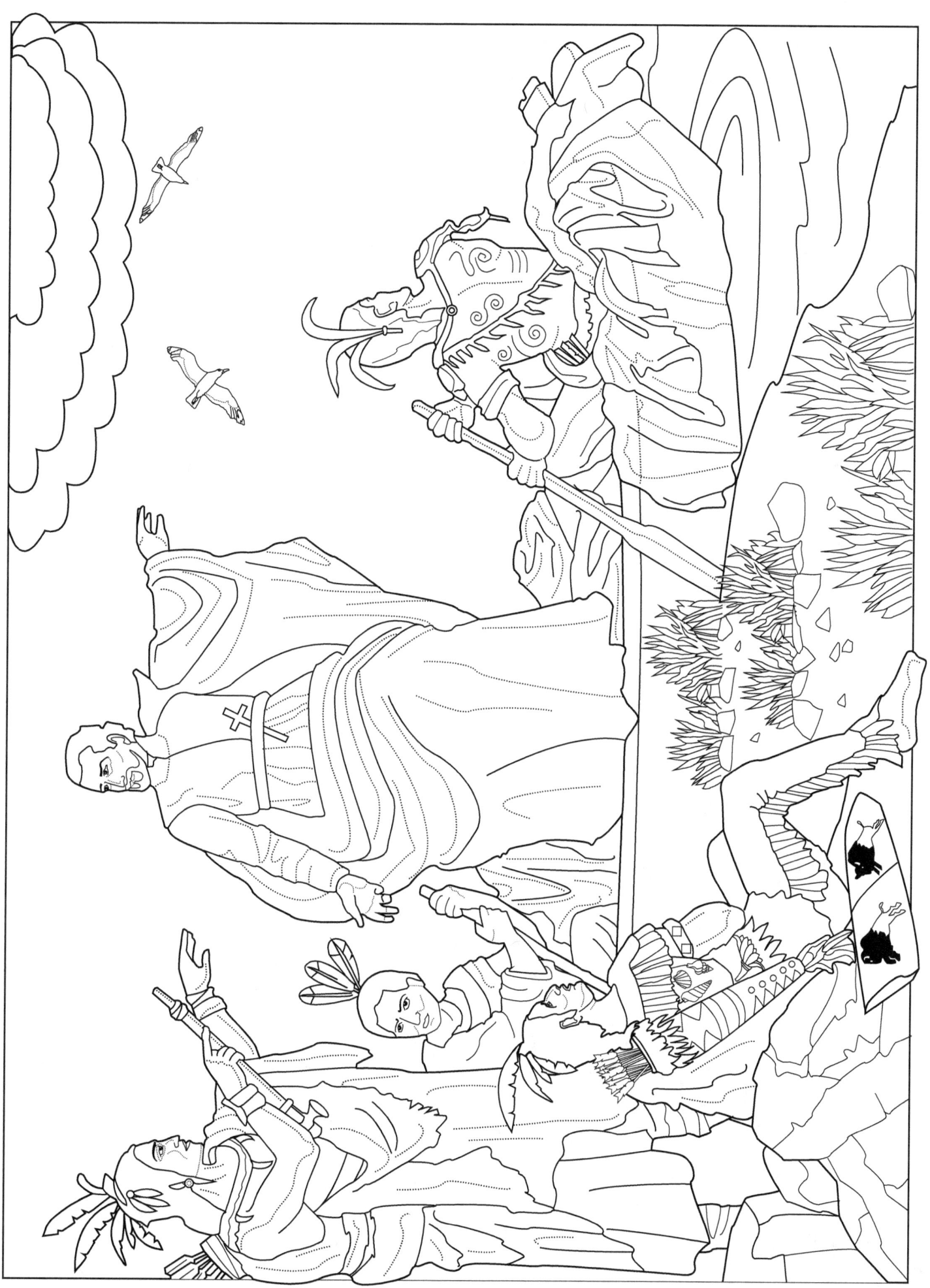